OTTO NICOLAI

THE MERRY WIVES
OF WINDSOR

Die lustigen Weiber
von Windsor
Les joyeuses commeres
de Windsor

Overture to the Opera

Ernst Eulenburg Ltd

London · Mainz · Madrid · New York · Paris · Prague · Tokyo · Toronto · Zürich

THE MERRY WIVES OF WINDSOR

WINDSOR

OVERTURE

Otto Nicolai.
1810-1849

2

Poco più animato.

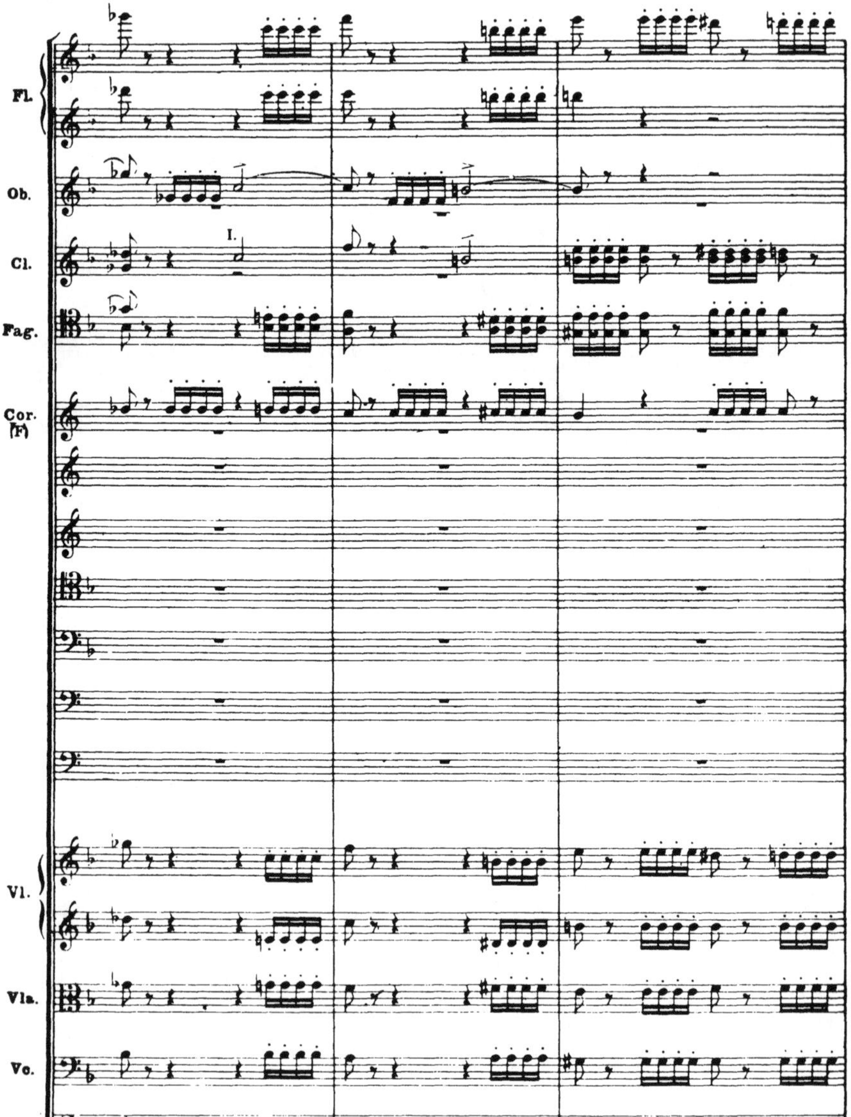
Fl.
Ob.
I.
Cl.
Fag.
Cor.
(F)
Vl.
Vla.
Vc.

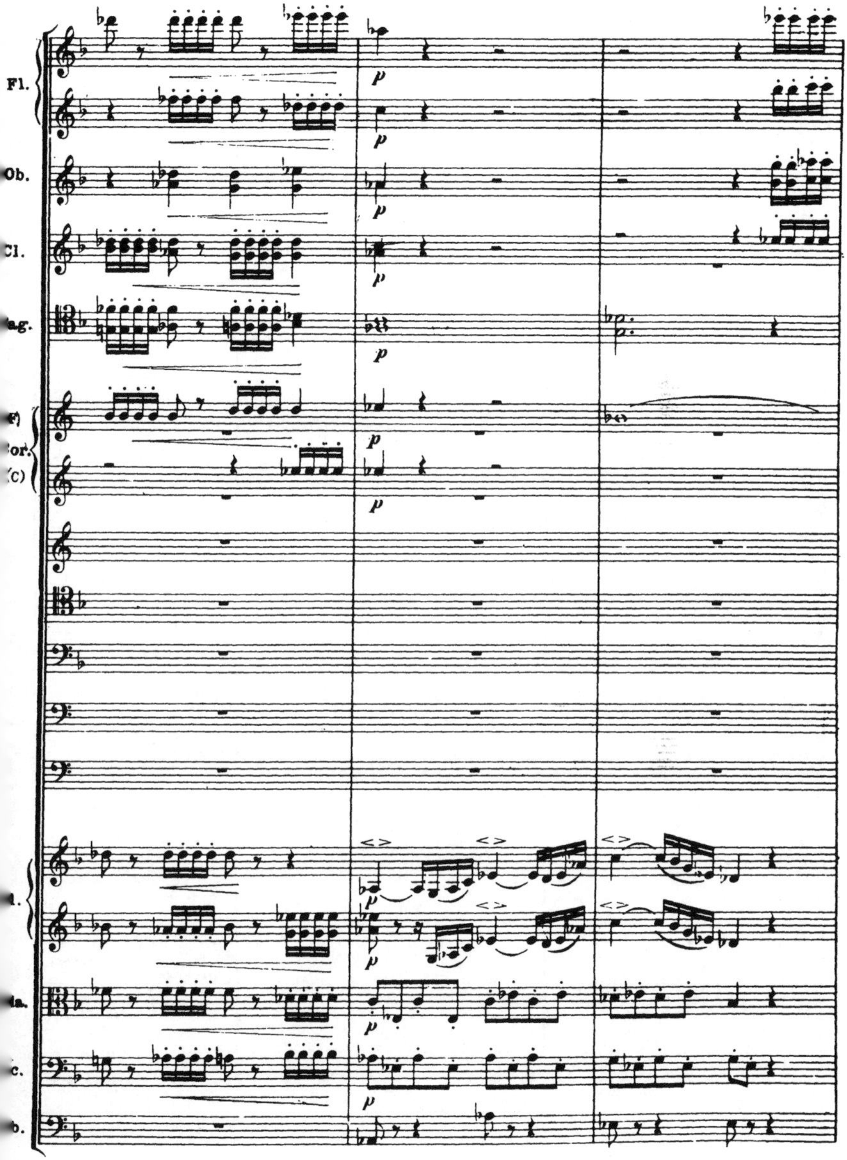
Fl.
Ob.
Cl.
ag.
F)
or.
(C)
l.
la.
c.
b.
p

poco rallent.

sempre più rallent.

Allegro vivace.

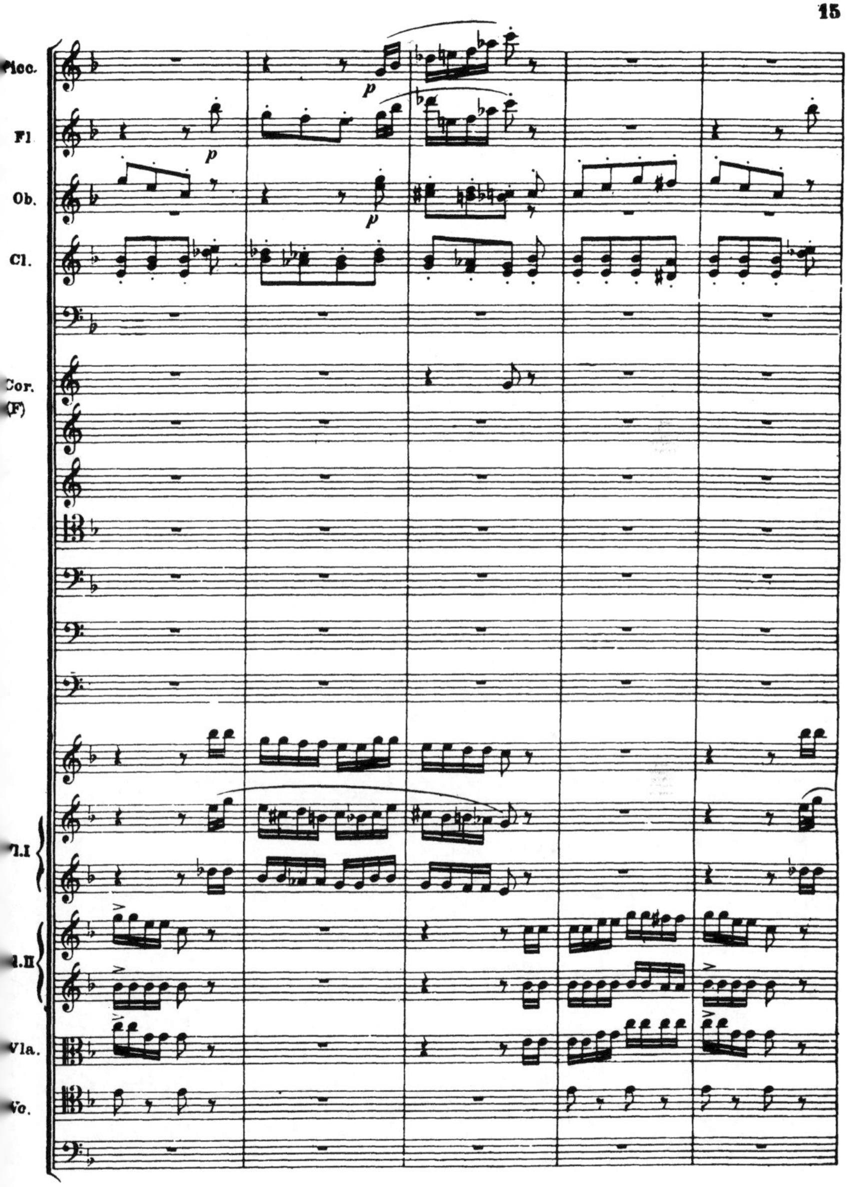
Fl
Ob.
Cl.
(F)
p
p
p

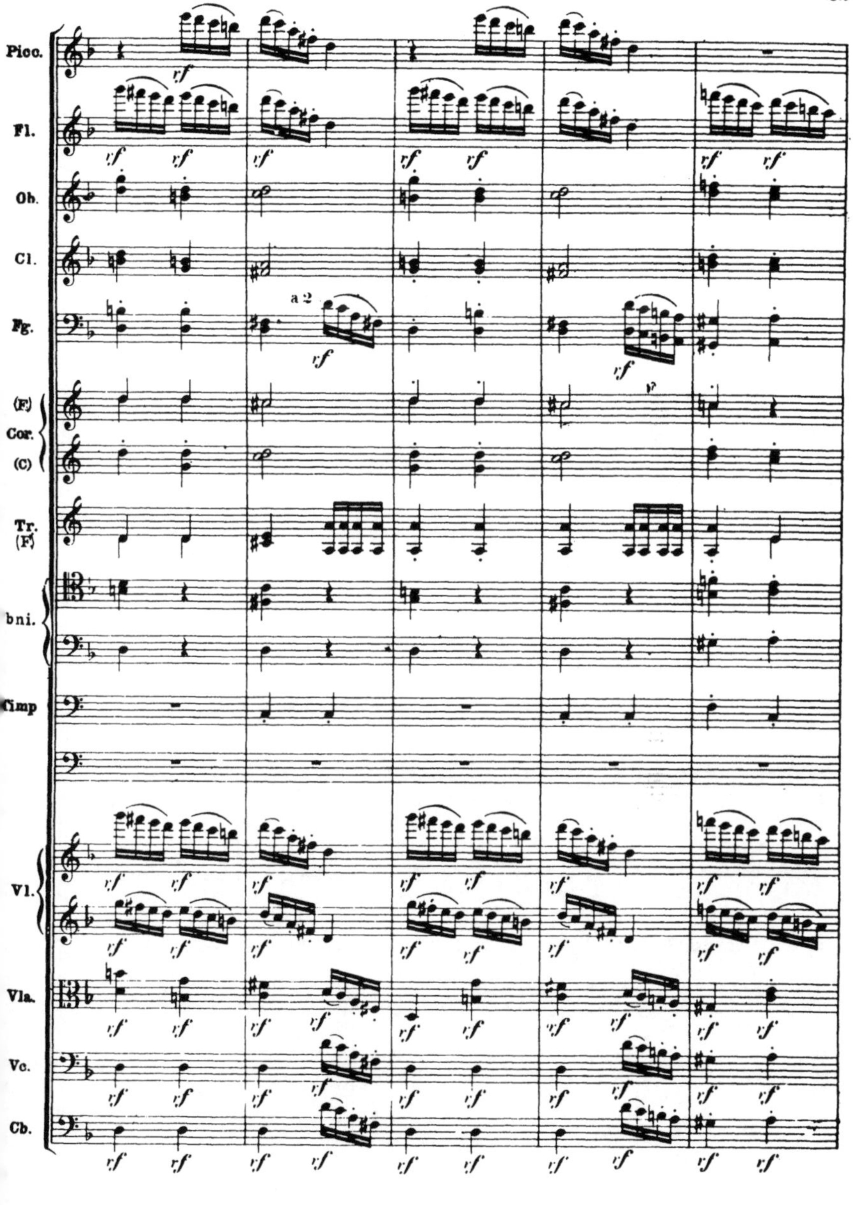
Picc.
Fl.
Ob.
Cl.
Fg.
a 2
(F)
Cor.
(C)
Tr.
(F)
bni.
Timp
Vl.
Vla.
Vc.
Cb.
rf

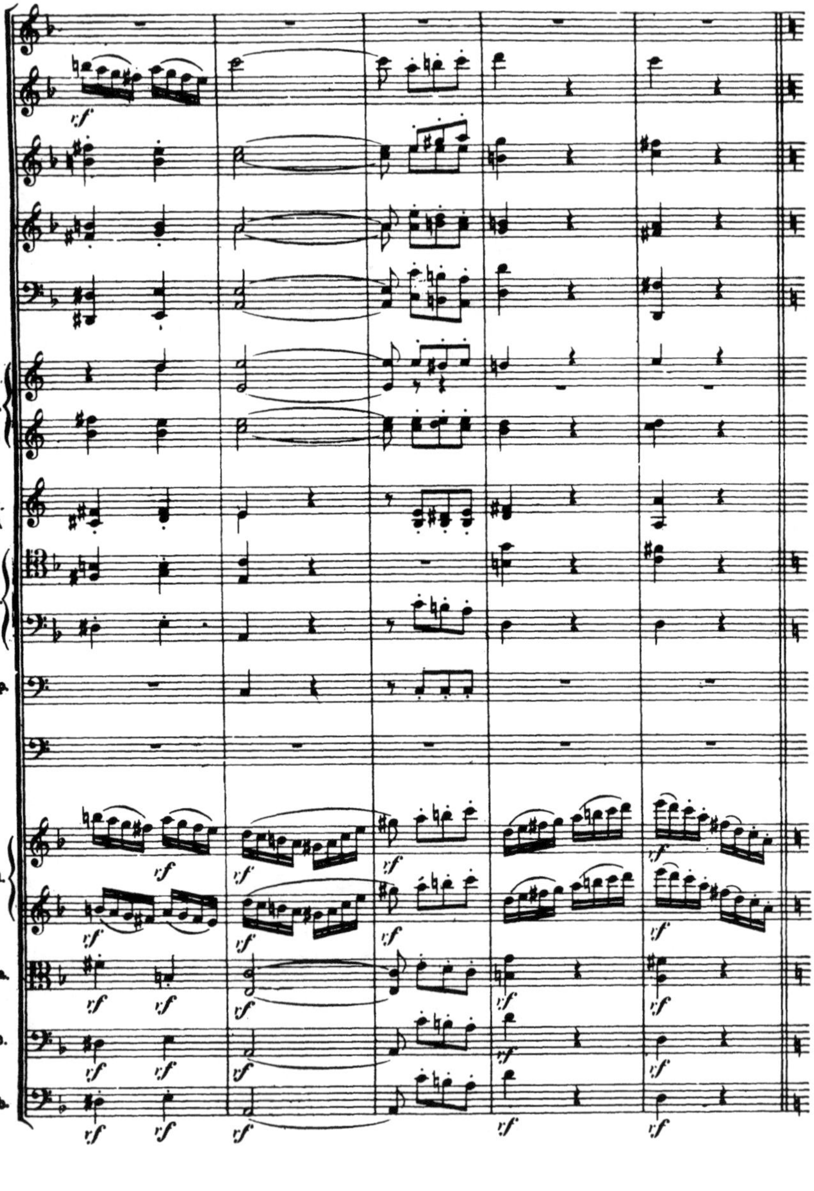
Fl.
Ob.
Cl.
Fg.
(F)
Cor.
(C)
Tr.
(F)
Tbni.
Timp.
Vl.
Vla.
Vc.
Cb.
rf

E.E. 3715

E.E. 3715

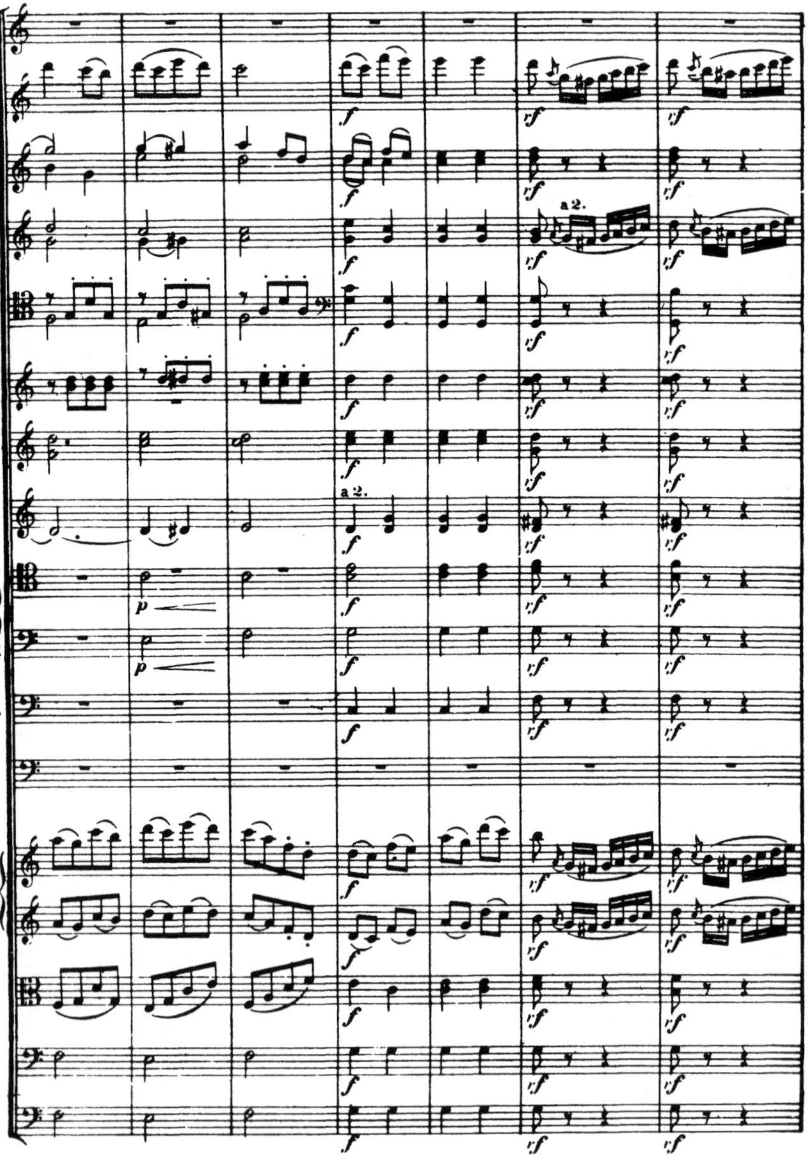

Fl.
Ob.
Cl.
a 2.
Fg.
(F)
Cor.
(C)
Tr
(F)
a 2.
bni.
Timp.
Vl.
Vla.
Vc.
Cb.

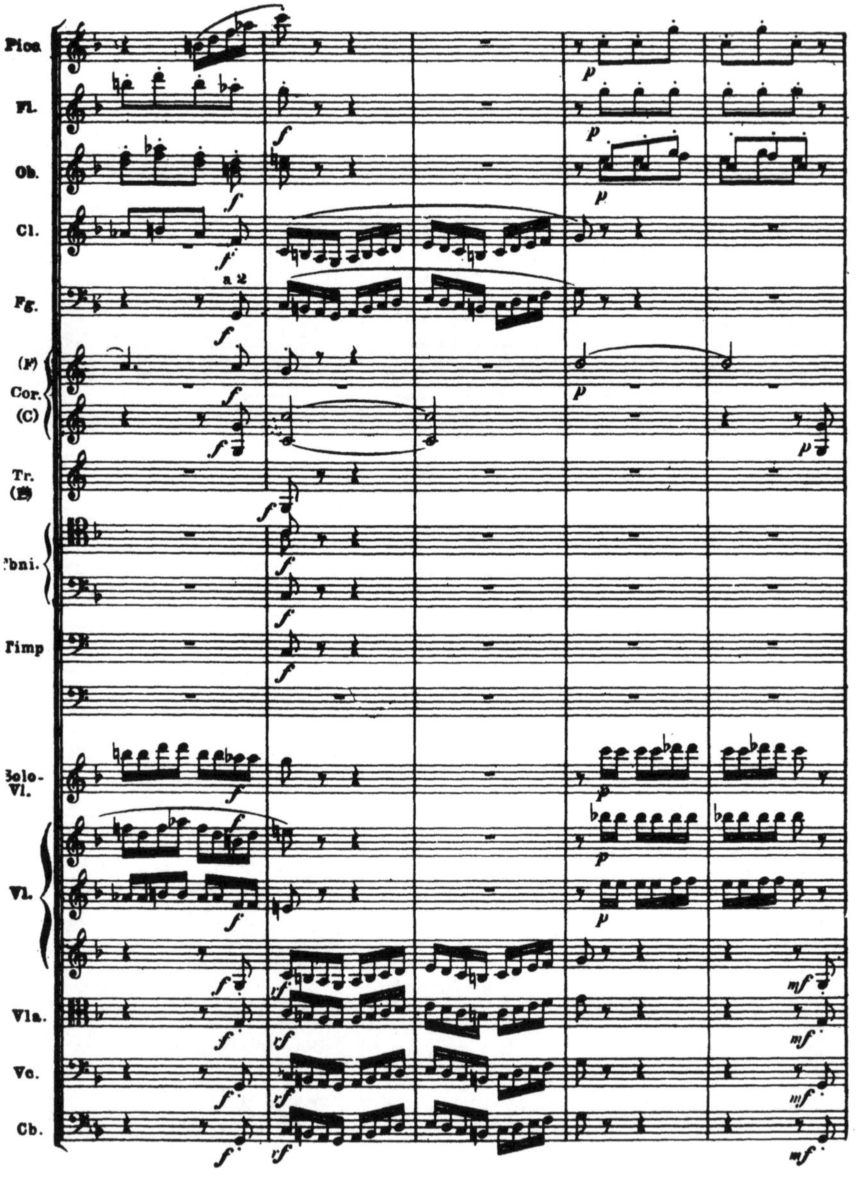
Picc.
Fl.
Ob.
Cl.
a 2
Fg.
Cor.
(C)
Tr.
Timp
Solo-Vl.
Vl.
Vla.
Vc.
Cb.

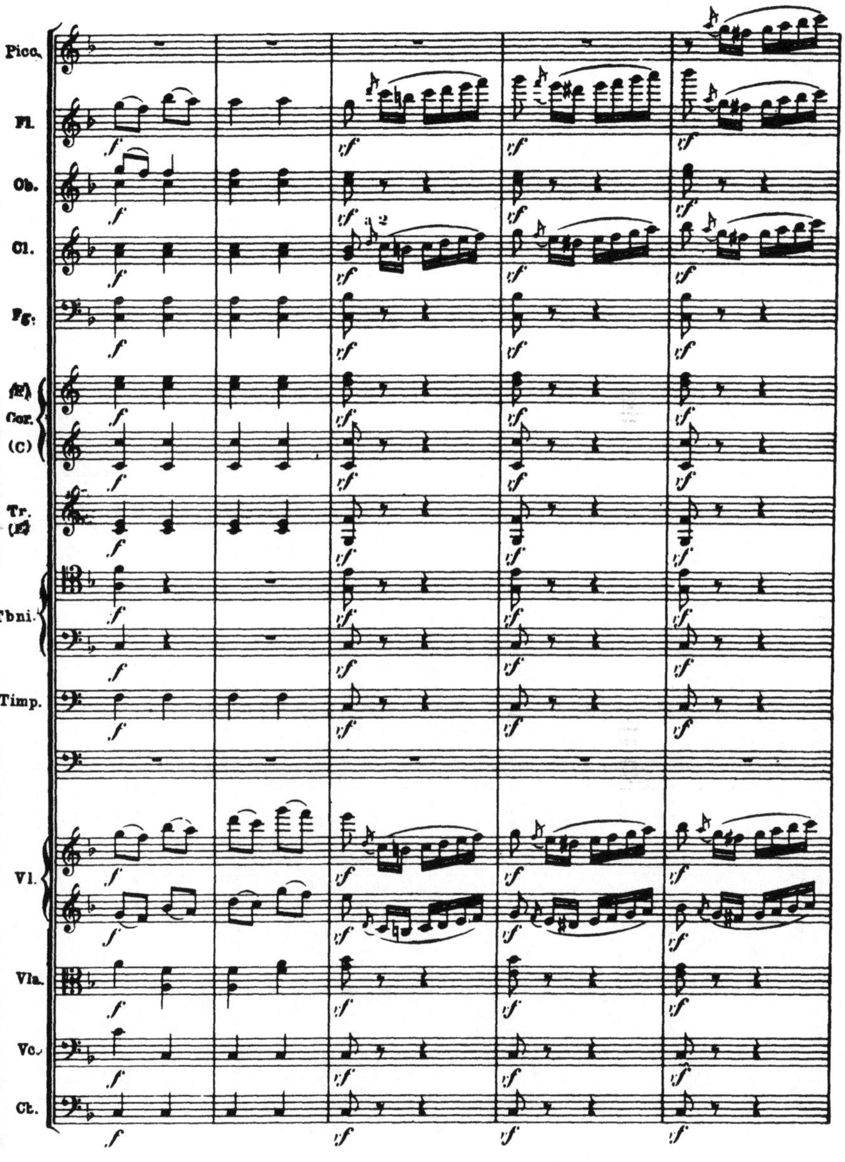
Picc.
Fl.
Ob.
Cl.
a 2
Fg.
(F)
Cor.
(C)
Tr.
(F)
Tbni.
Timp.
Vl.
Vla.
Vc.
Cb.

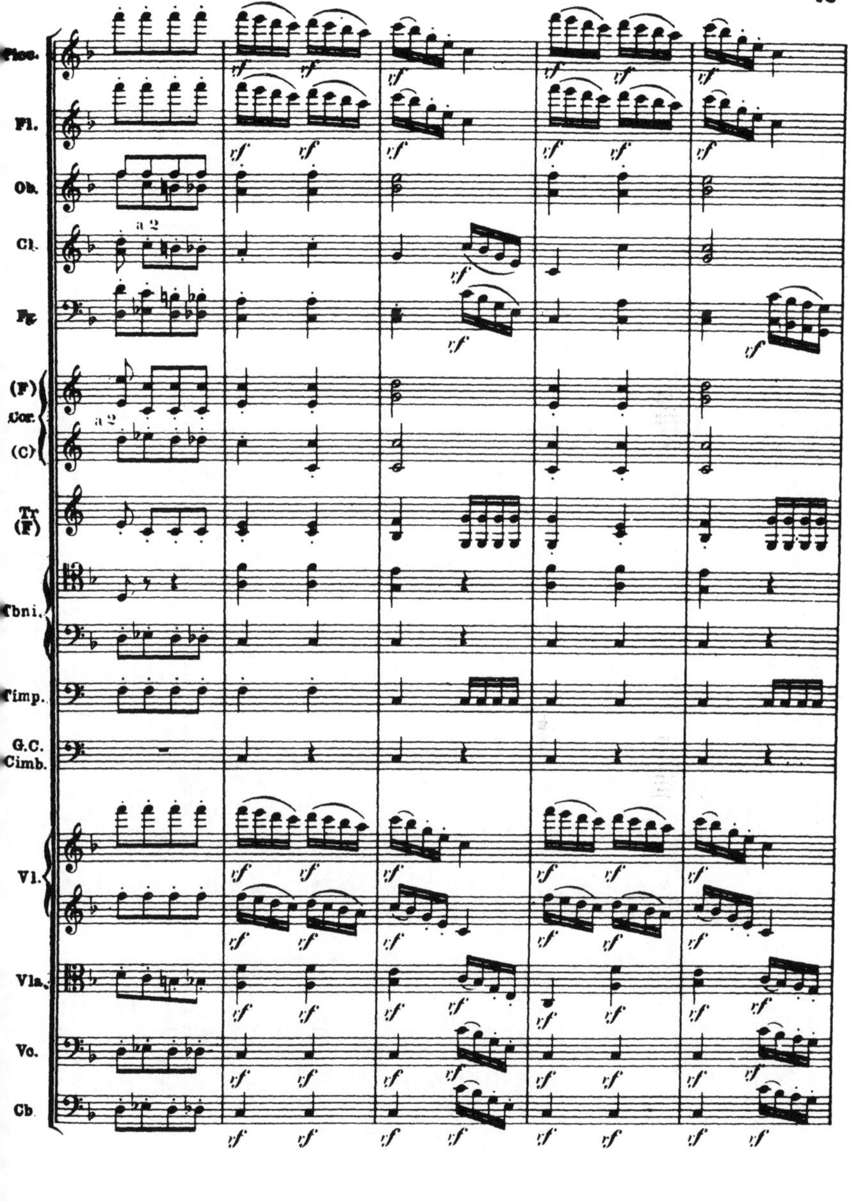

Picc.
Fl.
Ob.
Cl.
a 2
Fg.
(F)
Cor.
(C)
a 2
Tr. (F)
Tbni.
Timp.
G.C. Cimb.
Vl.
Vla.
Vc.
Cb.

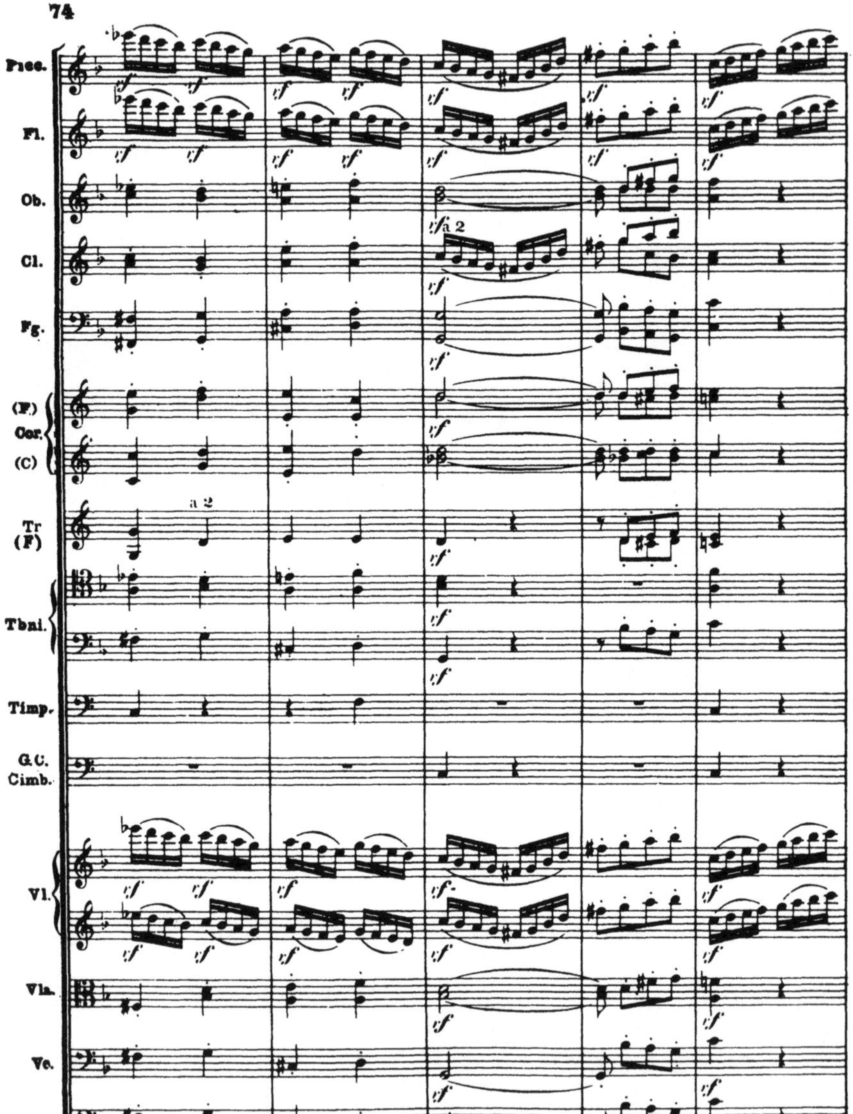
Picc.
Fl.
Ob.
Cl.
Fg.
(F)
Cor.
(C)
Tr
(F)
Tbni.
Timp.
G.C.
Cimb.
Vl.
Vla.
Vc.
Cb.
a 2
a 2

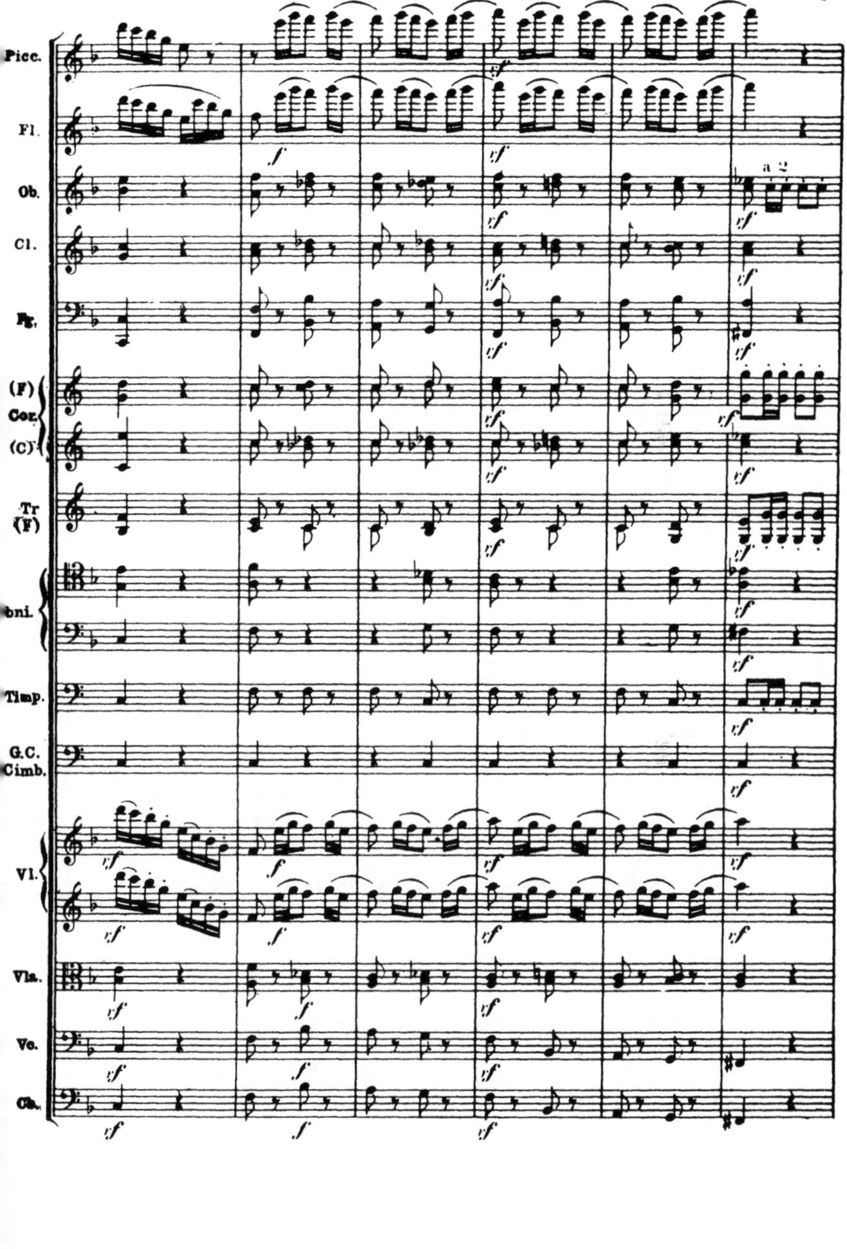
Picc.
Fl.
Ob.
Cl.
Fg.
(F) Cor. (C)
Tr (F)
bni.
Timp.
G.C. Cimb.
Vl.
Vla.
Vc.
Cb.
a 2
sf
f

Picc.
Fl.
Ob
Cl
Fg.
(F.)
Cor.
(C)
Tr.
(F)
Tbni.
Timp.
G.C.
Cimb.
Vl.
Vla.
Vc
Cb.
sf
ff
f
a 2